Celebrating Martin Luther King Jr. Day

Katie Peters

GRL Consultant Diane Craig,
Certified Literacy Specialist

Lerner Publications ◆ Minneapolis

Note from a GRL Consultant
This Pull Ahead leveled book has been carefully designed for beginning readers. A team of guided reading literacy experts has reviewed and leveled the book to ensure readers pull ahead and experience success.

Lerner Publications
An imprint of Lerner Publishing Group, Inc.
241 First Avenue North
Minneapolis, MN 55401 USA

For reading levels and more information, look up this title at www.lernerbooks.com.

Main body text set in Memphis Pro 24/39
Typeface provided by Linotype.

Photo Acknowledgments
The images in this book are used with the permission of: © Associated Press, pp. 3, 4–5, 16 (middle); © Jacob Lund/Shutterstock Images, 6–7; © Dmytro Zinkevych/Shutterstock Images, pp. 8–9, 16 (left); © antoniodiaz/Shutterstock Images, pp. 10–11, 16 (right); © Gene Herrick/Associated Press, pp. 12–13; © Jacob Lee Green/Sipa USA via AP, pp. 14–15.

Front Cover: © Horace Cort/Associated Press

Library of Congress Cataloging-in-Publication Data

Names: Peters, Katie author
Title: Celebrating Martin Luther King Jr. Day / written by Katie Peters.
Description: Minneapolis, Minnesota : Lerner Publications, [2026] | Series: Let's celebrate holidays (pull ahead readers—nonfiction) | Includes index. | Audience term: juvenile | Audience: Grades K–1 Lerner Publications | Audience: Ages 4–7 Lerner Publications | Summary: "On Martin Luther King Jr. Day we celebrate the man who taught us how to respect others. Engaging photographs give readers a glimpse into his life's work. Pairs with the story, Jade's Martin Luther King Jr. Day"—Provided by publisher.
Identifiers: LCCN 2024038504 (print) | LCCN 2024038505 (ebook) | ISBN 9798765668757 library binding | ISBN 9798765684443 paperback | ISBN 9798765678732 epub
Subjects: LCSH: Martin Luther King, Jr., Day—Juvenile literature | King, Martin Luther, Jr., 1929–1968—Juvenile literature | LCGFT: Biographies
Classification: LCC E185.97.K5 P438 2026 (print) | LCC E185.97.K5 (ebook) | DDC 323.092—dc23/eng

LC record available at https://lccn.loc.gov/2024038504
LC ebook record available at https://lccn.loc.gov/2024038505

Manufactured in the United States of America
1 – CG – 7/15/25

Table of Contents

Celebrating Martin Luther King Jr. Day

MLK Jr. is short for
Martin Luther King Jr.

He said to be kind.

He said to help others.

He said to share with others.

He worked to make
laws fair.

DR. MARTIN LUTHER
KING JR.
MARCH
THIS IS THRIVE

On MLK Jr. Day, we think of what he said. We think of what he did.

Did You See It?

help

MLK Jr.

share

Index